GREAT CLEAN JOKES FOR KIDS

Compiled and Edited by
DAN HARMON

A Barbour Book

© MCMXCVI by Barbour & Company, Inc.

ISBN 1-55748-904-1

Published by Barbour & Company, Inc.
P.O. Box 719
Uhrichsville, Ohio 44683
e-mail: books<barbour@tusco.net>

Member of the
Evangelical Christian
Publishers Association

Printed in the United States of America

GREAT CLEAN JOKES FOR KIDS

ANIMALS

What do you call a puppy who loves anchovies and garlic?
A dog whose bark is a thousand times worse than his bite.

Why do skunks smell so bad?
Cheap cologne.

Where do space explorers leave their space craft?
At parking meteors.

Why did the dog lie on its back with its feet sticking straight into the air?
It hoped to trip the birds.

What's minty, pasty, dangerous and kills germs?
Shark-infested toothpaste.

Why did the zoo veterinarian refuse to wear a necktie?
She already had a boa-tie.

Lorraine: "Did you know that your dog and my dog
are brother and sister?"
Larry: "Great! That means we're related!"

———

Why does a bear hibernate for three months
in cold weather?
We're all afraid to wake it up!

———

What kind of animal always is found
at baseball games?
The bat.

———

"Tracie's dog looks just like a member of her family," said Stacie.
"Which one?" asked Macie.

———

Why did the cow enroll in drama class?
To become a moo-vie star.

———

What keys are found in the animal kingdom?
Donkeys, monkeys and turkeys.

———

How do you snatch a rug from under a polar bear?
Wait 'til the bear migrates.

GREAT CLEAN JOKES FOR KIDS

What's a lamb's favorite department store?
Woolworth's.

———

Why do moose have fur coats?
They don't like wearing cotton.

———

Ingrid had caught a pond turtle and kept it in captivity for a couple of days, until her parents convinced her the little animal would be much happier in the wild. Her mother was very pleased when she saw Ingrid carrying the turtle out the back door.

"Where are you taking it?" her mother asked.

"Back to the pond."

"That's wonderful, Honey!"

But the next day, Ingrid's mother noticed the turtle was still around. She saw Ingrid walking out the front door with it in her palm.

"I thought you set the turtle free yesterday," her mother said.

"No, I just took it back to the pond for a visit. Today I'm taking it to the beach."

Mike: "I heard you got kicked out of the zoo last week."

Ike: "Yeah, for feeding the squirrels."

Mike: "Wow, I know they don't like for people to feed the animals, but that seems like strong punishment."

Ike: "Actually, I was feeding the squirrels to the cougars."

———

What did Natasha do when she found her pet dog eating her dictionary?
She took the words right out of his mouth.

———

"Did you know Bobby's in the hospital?" Tracie asked.

"No, what happened?" Laurie replied.

"He went to the zoo, and the zookeeper told him the alligator would eat off his hand. So he gave it a try."

———

Malcolm: "Dad, when you cut down a tree, isn't it true that a new tree sometimes grows out of the stump?"

Dad: "Yes, that's been known to happen."

Malcolm: "Then if you cut off my pony's tail, will a new pony grow out of the tail?"

Martha: "I hear you've been cruel to your cat."
Jeremy: "Nonsense. I simply twirl its tail around in the air occasionally."

———

What's black and white and furry and moves on 16 wheels?
A skunk on skates.

———

Lindsay: "Has is ever occurred to you that humans are the only animals who smoke cigarettes?"
Todd: "Well, we're the only animals who know how to strike matches."

———

Where's the best place to park dogs?
In a barking lot.

Maria: "I can always tell when my dog is happy."
Michael: "Does he wag his tail?"
Maria: "No, but he stops biting me."

———

How do you make a skunk stop smelling?
Cut off its nose.

———

Blake: "My dog's the smartest in town. He can say
his own name in perfect English."
Alice: "What's his name?"
Blake: "Ruff."

———

Why did the mouse give up tap dancing?
It kept falling into the sink.

———

What do you get when you cross a polar bear
and a sloth?
*A giant, white, furry animal that sleeps
while hanging upside-down from icicles.*

———

Why do coyotes call at night?
The rates are cheaper.

How do you catch a rabbit?
Hide in the bushes and sound like a carrot.

———

Nina: "I heard you just got back from Africa! Did you hunt wild game?"
Stevie: "Yeah, lions."
Nina: "Did you have any luck?"
Stevie: "Yep. Didn't see a one."

———

What's grey and has four legs and a trunk?
A mouse on vacation.

———

Why did the goat stick its head through the barbed wire fence?
To see what was on the other side.

———

What do you call a flying ape?
A hot-air baboon.

———

Why does the giraffe have a long neck?
So it won't have to smell its feet.

———

What kind of dog directs traffic?
A police dog.

How do you know if there's a bear in your toothpaste?

The toothbrush is too heavy to lift.

How do you save a hippopotamus drowning in hot cocoa?

Throw it a marshmallow.

A pet shop owner was trying to talk Mrs. McLellan into buying a dog for her children. "Oh, they'll love this little rascal!" said the clerk. "He's full of fun and he eats anything. He especially likes children."

What do you do when a mouse squeaks?

Oil it.

---

oinkment:
medicine for a pig with sore muscles.

What's black and white and has a red nose?

Rudolph the red-nosed zebra.

Why can't you telephone the zoo?

The lion's busy.

GREAT CLEAN JOKES FOR KIDS

What was the dog doing in the mud puddle?
Making mutt pies.

———

Tim: "I've heard bears won't chase you at night if you carry a flashlight."
Kim: "Depends on how fast you carry it."

———

What do rats keep in the glove compartments of their cars?
Rodent maps.

———

What was the turtle doing on the Los Angeles freeway?
Record time.

———

Teacher: If I give you four hamsters and your brother three hamsters, how many hamsters will you have altogether?
Student: Ten. We have three already.

What's green and white and green and white
and green and white?
An alligator somersaulting downhill.

What's the favorite city of hamsters?
Hamsterdam.

———

What's the favorite city of chickens?
Chicago.

———

Where do sheep get their hair cut?
At the baa-ber shop.

———

Why did the cow jump over the moon?
It forgot where it left its rocket ship.

———

What do you call a bull taking a nap?
A bulldozer.

———

How do you count a herd of cows?
With a cowculator.

Why doesn't the cow wear a bell?
Two horns are enough warning.

———

Where do cows go on dates?
To the moovies.

———

A flock of lambs were playing in the meadow. "Baa! Baa! Baa!" they called merrily—except one lamb who insisted, "Moo! Moo! Moo!"

"What are you saying?" they demanded.

"I'm practicing a foreign language."

———

Where do sheep go on vacation?
To the Baahaamaas.

———

Where does the farmer wash his livestock?
At the hogwash.

Sue: "Dogs are terrible dancers."
Allen: "How do you know that?"
Sue: "They have two left feet."

What did Shana say when his pet snake crawled
into the garbage disposal?
"It won't be long, now."

Bart: "Our house was robbed last night while we
were out."
Bret: "But I thought Butch was a great watchdog."
Bart: "Apparently he watched them take everything
in sight."

Why do firemen keep Dalmatians?
To find the fire hydrants.

Where do all the jungle animals like to eat lunch?
At the beastro.

What do you call a mild-mannered snake?
A civil serpent.

Police were investigating a break-in.

"Didn't you hear any strange noises next door last evening?" they asked one neighbor.

"We couldn't hear anything. Their dog was barking too loud."

———

What does a baby rattlesnake use for toys?
Its rattles.

———

Teacher: "Jerry, name an animal that's a carnivore."
Jerry: "A tiger."
Teacher: "That's good. Beryl, can you name a carnivore?"
Beryl: "Another tiger."

———

Rachel: "Did you know dogs eat more than elephants?"
Penny: "No way! How can they do that?"
Rachel: "There are thousands of times more dogs in the world than there are elephants."

———

Where do injured rabbits go?
To the hopspital.

ANTS & INSECTS

What's orange and has green spots, eight legs and one red eye?

I give up. What?

I don't know, but there's one crawling up your back.

How do you keep ants from digging mounds all over your yard?

Take away their shovels.

Why do spiders spin webs?

No one's ever taught them to crochet.

What do you get when you cross a tiger and a gnat?

A man-eating gnat.

Where do worms prefer to shop?
In the Big Apple.

Teacher: "The ant is a very industrious creature. It never seems to stop working—and do you see what it has to show for it?"
Student: "Yeah, it gets stepped on."

Two fleas hopped down the steps onto the sidewalk. One turned to the other and asked, "Should we walk, or take a dog?"

Jim and Ward were camping out one summer evening, and mosquitoes were a terrible problem. About dark, a different type of insect made its presence known: fireflies, darting here and there throughout the forest.

"Wow! Look at those mosquitoes!" cried Jim.

"Oh, no!" Ward said. "I thought we could hide from them in the dark, but they're coming after us with flashlights!"

Why did the flea work overtime?
It was saving up to buy a dog.

Why do hikers wear boots with ridged soles?
So ants will have an even chance.

Nell: "Is it true that ants are the hardest-working creatures?"

Science Teacher: "That's what a lot of scientists believe."

Nell: "Then why are they always attending picnics?"

Did the worms enter Noah's ark in pairs?
No, in apples.

AUTOMOBILES

Eve: "Is that a pleasant highway to drive on?"
Stevie: "No, it's a crossroad."

Why can't car mufflers participate
in marathon races?
They're too exhausted.

Maria: "What would you do if you were being chased by a runaway tractor-trailer truck at seventy miles an hour?"

Karl: "Eighty."

Why did the tire get fired from its job?
It couldn't stand the pressure.

———

Maggie and Sarah were driving to a party at a friend's house. The friend lived on a winding road off another winding road off another winding road in a very large neighborhood. Finally, they arrived.

"Well, I got us here," Maggie said, "but I may have to drive around awhile before I can find the right road home."

"Why can't you just put the car in reverse?" Sarah asked.

———

"What's wrong with your car?" a policeman asked as he approached a woman at roadside.

"I don't know. It just stopped running."

The policeman looked at the dashboard. "It's obviously out of gas," he said. "See? The needle is pointing to 'empty.'"

"Empty?" the woman said. "I thought the 'E' stood for 'enough.'"

———

"I wish I had enough money to buy a Rolls-Royce," Jory said.

"Why do you want a Rolls-Royce?" asked Floyd.

"I don't. It's the money I want."

BABIES

"What's your baby brother's name?"
"Don't know. He won't tell anybody."

Shirley: "I weighed only 2 pounds when I was born."
Ellen: "Wow! Did you survive?"

Student: "Were you ever a baby?"
Teacher: "Of course. Just like you were."
Student: "That's weird. I've never seen a baby teacher before."

Mother scolded her 2-year-old daughter, "Jacqueline, stop sucking your thumb."
"Why, Mommy?" little Jacqueline asked.
"It may be poisonous."

Kendall: "Mommy, there's a woman at the door with a baby."
Mommy: "Well, tell her we don't need anymore."

Liz: "We've found a way to keep my baby brother from spilling his food all over the table."

Melinda: "How?"

Liz: "We've started feeding him on the floor."

BIBLE JOKES

Who was the first tennis player in the Bible?
Joseph. He served in Pharoah's court.

———

Who was most sorry when the Prodigal Son returned home?
The fatted calf.

———

Sunday school teacher: "Nora, what does the Bible have to say about the Dead Sea?"

Nora: "Dead? I didn't even know it was ill!"

What kind of lights did Noah put on the ark?
Floodlights.

The Sunday School teacher asked her pupils to draw a picture of Joseph, Mary and the Christ child fleeing from Herod. Margie drew an airplane with three faces looking out the windows.

"That's interesting," the teacher said. "Where are they going?"

"Egypt," Margie replied.

"By airplane?"

"Yes. Pontius the pilot is driving."

Shelby: "Do you know at what point in history God created Eve?"

Sandra: "Right after He created Adam."

Alice: "Grandma, were you on Noah's ark?"
Grandma: "Oh, no."
Alice: "Then how did you survive the flood?"

What did Noah say when he'd finished loading the ark?
"Now I've herded everything."

BIRDS & BEES

What did the parrot say on Independence Day?
"Polly wanna firecracker."

———

Why won't you find much honey grown in Maryland?
There's only one "B" in Baltimore.

———

Brother: "It's a good thing you're not a swan."
Sister: "Why not?"
Brother: "You can't swim and you can't fly."

———

Why do hummingbirds hum?
They've never learned the words.

———

What's the easiest way to imitate a bird?
Eat worms.

———

Sissy: "Have you heard they're now making a special kind of ground meat out of bumblebees?"
Missy: "Yuk! What do they call that?"
Sissy: "Humburger."

Where do you treat an injured wasp?
At the waspital.

What goes "quick-quick?"
A duck with the hiccups.

Farmer Brown and Farmer Jones were sitting in front of the country store listening to the birds in the distance.

"There's an old owl," said Farmer Brown. "Can you hear it call, 'Hoo, hoo?'"

"That's not an owl," said Farmer Jones. "It's a dove. It's saying, 'Coo, coo.'"

Farmer Brown shook his head sadly. "I'm ashamed to say I know you. You don't recognize a 'hoo' from a 'coo.'"

Mickie: "My bulldog came away from the bird show with first prize."
Vickie: "How could a dog do that?"
Mickie: "He ate the winning parrot."

How do you tell a male robin from a female robin?
Call it by name. If he answers, it's a male.
If she answers, it's a female.

What do you call a duck's last will and testament?
A legal duckument.

Why do owls fly around at night?
It's faster than walking.

Bonnie: "Our parakeet bit my finger again this morning."
Benny: "Did you have to put anything on it?"
Bonnie: "Oh, no. He likes it plain."

Where on Noah's ark did the bees stay?
In the ark hives.

Where do ducks prefer to go on vacation?
The Duck-otas.

A band of pirates buried their treasure on the seashore. Afterward, they looked around for a marker but could find nothing except a few ostrich eggs. So they broke open the eggs, fried the yolks and left the shells on top of the buried treasure.

The pirate captain announced to his crew, "Eggs mark the spot."

What goes "peck-peck-peck-peck" and usually points to the north?
A magnetic woodpecker.

What do you call the Marines' pet bird?
A parrot trooper.

What do you get when you cross a parrot with a whippoorwill?
A bird that can sing both the words and the music.

Why did Judy keep her pet bird in a fish bowl?
The water wouldn't stay in a cage.

Where do wasps live?
Stingapore.

What do you say to a 200-pound parrot?
"Here's your box of crackers.
What else would you like?"

What kind of birds live in Central America?
Birds with suntans.

How can you tell a guy hummingbird
from a girl hummingbird?
By his mustache.

Candice: "I'm afraid to buy eggs at the supermarket,
because when I break them open at home I might
discover they have little chicks inside them."
Lennie: "Then why don't you buy goose eggs?"

What parrot was a famous Antarctic explorer?
Admiral Bird.

What's the favorite sport of platypuses?
Bill-iards.

BOOKS

Mitzy: "I just read a very stirring book."
Gordon: "What was it about?"
Mitzy: "Cooking."

Little Lauren stomped up to the return desk at a department store. "Is it really true you'll give me a refund if I'm not fully satisfied with one of your products?" she asked the clerk.

"Certainly," said the clerk.

"Good," Lauren said, putting a new paperback novel on the counter. "I bought this here last week, and I don't like the ending."

A man in a bookstore wanted to buy a book titled *How to Become a Billionaire Overnight.* But some of the pages were missing, so he complained to the shop owner.

"What's the problem?" asked the owner. "You'll still become at least a millionaire."

CHICKEN JOKES

Who was the least favorite president of chickens?
Herbert Hoover.
"A chicken in every pot," he promised.

Why did the chicken cross the road?
To avoid Colonel Sanders.

Why did the chewing gum cross the road?
It was stuck to the bottom of the chicken's shoe.

Why did the farmer cross the road?
To catch his chickens.

What's the best way to move a chicken?
Pullet.

Why did the brontosaurus cross the road?
Chickens had not been invented.

Why do chickens have short legs?
So the eggs won't break as they're laid.

"I don't like my job," grumbled the first rooster.
"Why not?" asked the second rooster.
"I'm working for chicken feed."

Why do you never see chickens at the zoo?
They prefer the museum.

Who is the favorite actor of chickens?
Gregory Peck.

Why did the chicken go to New York City?
To visit the Henpire State Building.

A chicken went to the doctor.
"What's your problem?" the doctor asked.
"I have red, puffy spots all over my skin."
"Oh, no! You have the people pox!"

Why did the rooster cluck at midnight?
His cluck was fast.

———

What did the Navy get when it crossed a chicken
with a case of dynamite?
A mine layer.

———

Farmer: "Why aren't we having eggs for breakfast
this morning?"
Farmer's wife: "I think the chicken mislaid them."

———

What is the favorite musical of chickens?
Fiddler on the Roost.

———

How does a chicken farmer wake up
in the morning?
Probably with an alarm clock.

———

Why did the rock band hire a chicken?
They needed the drumsticks.

———

How do you catch a chicken?
Hide in the yard and act like a corn kernel.

How do chickens stay warm?
With their central bleating system.

Why was the chicken sitting on the eggplant?
She was near-sighted.

THE CIRCUS

Why did the knife swallower swallow
an umbrella?
*She wanted to put something
away for a rainy day.*

———

Lorrie: "Did you hear about the circus sword swallower being arrested?"
Rory: "No, what happened?"
Lorrie: "She burped and stabbed somebody in the audience."

CLOTHES

"Lane, look at you!" shrieked his mother. "You've ruined your brand new suit falling into the mud!"

"I'm sorry," Lane said. "I didn't have time to take it off before I hit the water."

———

Why did Christy put on a wet dress?

Because the label said "Wash and Wear."

———

Sherie: "Mommy, can I try on that dress in the window?"

Mother: "No, you'll have to go to the dressing room."

Missy: "I just got a new pair of alligator shoes!"
Sissy: "I didn't know you had an alligator."

———

Wren: "Don't you realize your umbrella has a hole in it?"
Adrienne: "Sure. It lets me check and see when the rain stops."

———

Polly: "Why are you wearing all those clothes to go paint the fence?"
Agnes: "The can says you need two coats to do a good job."

CRAZY FOLKS

Susan: "We have a terrible problem. Our mother thinks she's a chicken."
Wanda: "Why don't you take her to a psychiatrist?"
Susan: "We need the eggs."

———

Why did the woman remove her nose?
To see what made it run.

Why did the carpenter put his finger over the head
of the nail he was hammering?
To muffle the noise.

———

Dennis: "Steve's changed his mind again."
Suzanne: "Well, I hope this one's got more sense
than the last one he had."

———

Warren: "Lester sure has a weird sense of humor."
Katrina: "How so?"
Warren: "We went into an antique shop yesterday,
and he asked the owner, 'What's new?'"

———

Why did the neighbor peek over the brick fence?
Because he couldn't see through it.

———

"Veronica has got to be the nicest person ever born,"
said Andrew.
"What makes you think so?" asked Arthur.
"She says 'thank you' to automatic sliding doors."

———

Ray: "It's dark in here. Strike a match."
Roy: "I'm trying to, but this match won't light."
Ray: "Is it wet?"
Roy: "I don't think so. It worked a minute ago."

Michael: "Why are you making faces at my dog? That's silly."
Mort: "Why thank you. I picked it myself."

Wil: "You have a stately nose, sir."
Artie: "Well, he started it."

Dallas: "Tony sure has a mind of his own."
Alice: "I don't think anybody else really wants it."

———

"My son thinks he's a dog. He barks at people and chases cars and cats."
"How long has he behaved this way?"
"Basically, since he was a puppy."

———

Melissa: "I think Cathy's a little distracted. She sure is wasting a lot of money."
Sandi: "Oh? How?"
Melissa: "Well, for example, she's been going to a lot of drive-in movies lately."
Sandi: "That sounds pretty normal to me—and cheap."
Melissa: "But she takes a taxi."

DEFINITIONS

archaeologist: a scientist whose life is in ruins.

atom: Eve's husband.

autobiography: a book about a car.

bookkeeper: a person who doesn't return library books on time.

bowling balls: what elephants use for marbles.

cartoon: a song about an automobile.

cashew: the way nuts sneeze.

catsup: what you have to do when you're behind.

Cheerios: what tiny people use for life preservers.

Cheerios: donut seeds.

chipmonk: a monkey eating potato chips.

circle: a line that meets its other end in secret.

commentator: an every-day potato.

coquette: a small cola.

dentist's office: a filling station.

disease: de seven big bodies of water where de ships sail.

dogwood: the tree with the loudest bark.

don't: short for "doughnut."

drydock: a thirsty surgeon.

enormous: a very large moose.

footnote: a sound you play with your feet.

frozen police officers: copsicles.

hippie: what holds up your leggie.

horse doctor: a doctor with a sore throat.

humbug: a roach who loves music.

lambchops: the way sheep cut their firewood.

lemonade: helping a lemon cross the street.

mischief: the police chief's wife.

mountain range: a cook stove inside a cabin in the Rockies.

mushroom: the room where Eskimos train their sled dogs.

panther: a person who manufactures panths.

pineapple: the fruit of a pine tree.

pocket calculator: a device for counting pockets.

polygon: a deceased parrot.

raisin: a worried grape.

short-order cook: a person who prepares food for children.

stagecoach: a theatrical instructor.

stucco: what happens when you step on a piece of used bubblegummo.

Sugar Bowl: where flies play championship foot ball.

Super Bowl: swimming pool for Superman's gold fish.

teacher's pet: student of a teacher who can't afford a cat.

thumb tacks: a tax on thumbs.

toadstool: a place for a frog to sit down.

unaware: what you put on first and take off last.

watershed: a haven for ships in the middle of the ocean.

venison: a type of meat that costs deerly.

vipers: the things that keep car vindows clear ven ever it rains.

waterbed: where fish sleep.

zebra: a horse in prison.

zinc: what happens to you in the water if you can't zwim.

DOCTORS

What do you call a surgeon with eight arms?

A doctopus.

———

Patient: "Doc, can you make house calls?"
Doctor: "That depends. How sick is the house?"

———

What did the doctor say to the woman who swallowed a spoon?

"*Sit still and don't stir.*"

What kind of people enjoy bad health?
Doctors.

Doctor: "I want you to drink plenty of liquids so you'll get over this cold."
Mrs. Martin: "I never drink anything else."

What do you call foot X-rays?
Footographs.

A woman barged into a doctor's office and demanded attention. "I dreamed I ate a giant marshmallow!" she screamed.
"Control yourself," said the receptionist. "It was only a dream."
"No dream! When I woke up, my pillow was missing!"

What do you call a bone specialist from Egypt?
A Cairopractor.

How is a surgeon like a comedian?
They both keep you in stitches.

Eye Doctor: "You need a new pair of glasses."
Patient: "How do you know that? You haven't examined me yet."
Doctor: "Because you just came in through my office window."

Woman: "My husband snores so loudly he keeps everybody in the house awake. What can we do?"
Doctor: "Try turning him on his side, massaging his shoulders and neck, and stuffing a washcloth into his mouth."

ELEPHANTS

Why are elephants so wrinkled?
They stay in the bathtub too long.

Why are elephants so wrinkled?
They're too difficult to iron.

What's big and grey and has a trunk and goes "zrrrrrrrrrr?"
An outboard elephant.

How do elephants communicate?
With elephones.

Why are elephants grey?
So you can tell them from bananas.

How do you make an elephant float?
Start with your favorite ice cream,
pour cola over it and add elephant.

Why was the elephant wearing a purple T-shirt?
His other shirts were all at the cleaners.

Why is a snail small and smooth?
Because if it were huge and wrinkled,
it would be an elephant.

What's the best way to tell a kitten
from an elephant?
Try picking it up. If it's too heavy,
it's surely an elephant.

What's the difference between an elephant in
Africa and an elephant in India?
Several thousand miles.

How do you treat an elephant with seasickness?
Give it a lot of space.

———

What's the difference between Superman
and an elephant?
The elephant wears a big "E" on his chest.

FARM JOKES

One rooster said to another, "You don't want to mess
with the new rooster in the yard. He's mean."
"How do you know?" asked the second rooster.
"He came from a hard-boiled egg."

———

What did the farmer say to the sheep?
"Hey, ewe!"

———

Why did the farmer put razor blades
in the potato patch?
He wanted to grow potato chips.

Why did the farmer spend the day
stomping his field?
He wanted mashed potatoes.

Farmer: "You know, the people in my little town are smarter than the people in your big city."
City Feller: "How do you get that?"
Farmer: "We know where LA is, but you don't know where Podunk is."

Mary was visiting her grandparents on the farm. "That little pig sure eats a lot of corn," she said.
"He has to make a hog of himself," said Grandmother, "or he'll never be full-grown."

What did the farmer say to the hayfield?
I'm very sorry, but I have to mow now.

First farmer: "Did the tornado damage your barn last night?"
Second farmer: "I don't know. Haven't found it yet."

What did the farmer do at the chocolate factory?
Milk chocolates.

What did the pea patch say to the corn patch?
Stop stalking me.

———

Why did the farmer raise his children in a barn?
*He wanted them to grow up
in a stable environment.*

———

Betsy and Pat were roaming the meadows of their grandparents' farm when they encountered a dangerous-looking bull.

"Are you afraid?" asked Pat.

"Not me," said Betsy. "I'm a vegetarian."

———

Why did the farmer buy an automatic calculator?
To see if his livestock would multiply faster.

———

Elaine: "My uncle just bought a farm that's a mile long and an inch wide.

Penny: "What does he think he can grow on land like that?"

Elaine: "Spaghetti, I guess."

———

When do you hear the shout,
"Ready. . . . Set. . . . Hoe?"
At the beginning of a race between two farmers.

Robby: "What would you do if a bull charged?"
Toby: "I'd give him all the time he wanted to pay off the bill."

FOOD

What did one hot dog say to the other?
"Frankly, I prefer cheeseburgers."

One Irish potato said to the other Irish potato, "I'm about to change my nationality."
"How are you going to do that?"
"By becoming French fries."

What's the difference between an Oreo cookie and a cheeseburger?
Oreos taste much better dunked in milk.

How do you tell a chili pepper from a bell pepper?
The chili pepper always wears a jacket.

Ingrid: "Do you know what makes the Tower of Pisa lean?"
Peter: "It's malnourished, I guess."

How do you deliver fried pies to customers?
On piecycles.

What's the difference between a jar of peanut butter
and a freight train?
*A freight train doesn't stick
to the roof of your mouth.*

What did one cannibal say to the other
as they gobbled up a clown?
"This food tastes funny."

Muldrow: "When did Caesar utter the famous state-
ment, 'Et tu, Brute'?"
Muldoon: "When Brutus asked him how many
cheeseburgers he'd had at the cookout."

Why was Miss Muffet reading a map?
Because she'd lost her whey.

Father: "It's proper manners to eat your food with
your fork, not your spoon."
Marvin: "But my fork leaks."

What's the favorite food of Martians?
Martianmallows.

What do you get if you cross a bulldog with a bull?
A burger that can bite back.

How can you tell if a rattlesnake has been drinking your milk?
By the two fang marks in the carton.

What did the Gingerbread Man do when his eyesight failed?
Bought contact chocolate chips.

What did the butcher get when he crossed a chicken with King Kong?
A giant drumstick.

Coreen: "I ate a yo-yo lunch."
Sonny: "What's a yo-yo lunch?"
Coreen: "Soon after you get it down, it comes up again."

51

What's the favorite lunch item in Iceland?

Chili dogs.

Teacher: "Marvin, you haven't washed. I can see food on your face."

Marvin: "What food?"

Teacher: "The eggs you had for breakfast this morning."

Marvin: "Eggs? I had cereal for breakfast this morning. The eggs must be from yesterday morning."

Why did the tangerine go to the movies alone?

It couldn't find a date.

What happened when Grandma served ostrich instead of turkey for Thanksgiving dinner?

It buried its head in the pumpkin pie.

Maria: "You can have my M&Ms."

Alex: "You don't like candy?"

Maria: "Not this kind. Too hard to peel."

GREAT CLEAN JOKES FOR KIDS

Thomas: "Gerald sure does love Chinese food."
Veronica: "Yeah, I think he's a chow meiniac."

Chris: "I have to eat very balanced meals."
Burt: "I didn't know you were so health-conscious."
Chris: "I'm not, really. I'm training to be a tightrope walker."

A prospector straggled into town, went into the little café and told the owner, "Buddy, I'm starved almost to death. It's been two weeks since I've tasted food."

The bartender responded, "Well, it all tastes about the same as it did back then."

René: "How do you like those crabapples?"
Richard: "They taste rather salty, for apples."

FROGS

What goes "CROAK! CROAK!"
on foggy nights?
A froghorn.

What's green and stands in a corner?
A frog that got caught talking in class.

Where do frogs hang their coats?
In the croakroom.

What's white on the outside, green on the inside and
makes croaking sounds?
A frog sandwich.

Where do frogs fly their flags?
On tadpoles.

GROWN-UPS

"I think my father's getting old," Keri lamented.
"What makes you think so?" asked Janelle.
"It takes him more time to rest up than it does to
get tired."

Why did Mommy tip-toe past
the medicine cabinet?
She didn't want to wake up the sleeping pills.

"Grandpa, why don't you ever read the newspaper?"
"I don't want to put any needless wear on my
spectacles."

Patti: "How do you do today?"
Grumpy Grandpa: "How do I do what?"

Grandma was giving Sarah some wise advice:
"Never put off until tomorrow what you can do
today. Do you understand what I mean?"
"Yes, Grandma. It means we should finish this
apple pie right now."

Don: "My parents once crossed the Atlantic with
Elizabeth on the Queen Elizabeth II."
Dean: "You mean they got to know the queen?"
Don: "No, they were with my Grandmother
Elizabeth."

Kendra: "Martin, what will you do when you grow
up to be as big as your daddy?"
Martin: "Go on a diet, first of all."

David: "My dad never gets his hair wet when he showers."
Nan: "Does he wear a shower cap?"
David: "Nope. He's bald."

———

Sally: "My mother has trained herself to walk in her sleep every night."
Cal: "Why would she want to do that?"
Sally: "To save time. This way she can get her exercise and her rest all at once."

———

Bailey: "Why does your dad wrap newspapers all over himself?"
Barry: "He likes to dress with *The Times*."

———

"I don't think my mom is a very smart parent," Jill said.
"Why not?" asked Grace Ann.
"She's always sending me to bed when I'm not sleepy and making me get up when I'm still tired."

———

Mother: "Troy, I've been calling you for the last five minutes! Didn't you hear me?"
Troy: "No, I didn't hear you until the fourth time you called."

Some grown-ups are as hard to wake up as sleeping bags.

———

Brooke: "Why is your father always flying his airplane?"
Ellie: "He says a space shuttle would cost too much money."

———

Mother: "Stan, wash your face."
Stan: "It's not fair."
Mother: "What do you mean?"
Stan: "Dad has less to wash because of his beard."

———

Sal: "I can't think of a good present for Mom on Mother's Day."
Val: "Why not lipstick?"
Sal: "Nah. . . . I'm not sure what size her mouth is."

———

"I figured out how to make my dad laugh Sunday."
"Really? How?"
"I told him a joke Friday."

———

Rachel: "Do you know the difference between Daddy's toys and Brother's toys?"
Fran: "Yeah, Daddy's cost a lot more money."

Earl: "Wanna know a funny coincidence about my parents?"

Virl: "Sure. What?"

Earl: "They were both married at the same time, same day, same year—and same place!"

"Do you get spanked much?" a child asked his friend.

"Yes. I think I'm the kind of boy my parents don't want me to play with."

"My grandmother is always complaining about how awful it feels to be old," Carmen said.

"Mine, too," said Dixie. "I guess those wrinkles hurt a lot."

HISTORY

Why did Columbus sail to America?
It was faster than swimming.

Why did the Romans build straight roads?
*So their enemies couldn't hide
around the curves.*

Teacher: "How long did the Hundred Years' War last?"

Student: "I don't know. Ten years?"

Teacher: "No! Think carefully. How old is a 5-year-old horse?"

Student, thoughtfully: "Oh, 5 years old!"

Teacher: "That's right. So how long did the Hundred Years' War last?"

Student: "Now I get it—5 years!"

Why did cave men live in caves?

They couldn't afford condominiums.

History Teacher: "What English monarch was also an amateur doctor?"

Jamie: "William the Corn Curer?"

Teacher: "What was the Romans' most famous achievement?"

Pupil: "They could read Latin."

The teacher held up a picture of Abraham Lincoln and asked the class, "Can anyone tell me who this is?"

"I know!" shouted Mindy. "He's the man who owns all the pennies."

History Teacher: "Now Wally, what can you tell us about President Millard Fillmore?"

Wally: "He's dead."

A history teacher was discussing the early American explorers. "Merrivale the Monk spent years living with the native Americans, learning their songs," she said. "The Indians gave him a special name. Do you know what it was, Jack?"

"Tone-Deaf," guessed Jack.

William: "Did you hear the North and South are going to refight the Battle of Kennesaw Mountain?"
Wade: "What for?"
William: "Because it wasn't fought on the level the first time."

Where did Lincoln sign the Emancipation Proclamation?
At the bottom of the last page.

Lana: "My great-great-great-grandparents were the first citizens of this town."
Kurt: "That's nothing. My ancestors fought in the Revolutionary War."
Lana: "My ancestors fought in ancient Rome."
Kurt: "My ancestors fought for Alexandar the Great before that."
Lana: "My ancestors were on the ark with Noah."
Kurt: "My ancestors had their own ship."

Teacher: "Who won at Bull Run?"
Student: "Was that a tennis match or a horse race?"

Baker: "I wish I'd been born about 4,000 years ago."
Brewster: "Why?"
Baker: "So I wouldn't have to learn so much history."

What do history teachers talk about
when they get together?
The old days.

———

How did the ancient Vikings communicate?
Norse Code.

———

Teacher: "What do you think George Washington
would say about America if he were alive today?"
Student: "Doesn't matter. He would be so old, his
ideas would be completely useless."

HOUSES

Marcia: "How do you like your new house?"
Kyle: "It's okay, but kinda small. We had to
remove the paint from the walls in order to make all
our furniture fit."

———

Dee Dee: "Did you know Santa Claus has a secret
fear of crawling down chimneys?"
Pee Wee: "No! Is he afraid of closed-in places?"
Dee Dee: "Yes. It's called Claustrophobia."

Two carpenters were building a house. One examined every nail before using it and ended up throwing half of them away.

"Why are you wasting those nails?" his partner asked.

"They're no good. The sharp points are on the wrong end."

"Yeah, but you could use those for the other side of the house."

HUNTING & FISHING

Game Warden: "You're under arrest. You're hunting with last year's license."

Hunter: "But I'm only trying to shoot the deer that got away last year."

———

What did the free fish say to the fish that just got hooked?

Shoulda kept your mouth shut like I told you."

———

"I'm not going fishing with my little brother ever again," Roy said.

"Why not?" asked Rob. "Does he move around too much at the edge of the water?"

"No. He eats all the worms."

KITCHEN JOKES

Ginger: "Mommy, I need another glass of milk."
Mommy: "You've had two already. Why are you so thirsty this morning?"
Ginger: "I'm not. I'm checking to see if my throat leaks."

———

Mother: "Joy, haven't you finished making the Kool-Aid yet?"
Joy: "I'm having trouble getting the water into the envelope."

———

How can you tell if there's a horse
in your refrigerator?
By the hoof prints in the butter.

———

Paul: "Why are you staring at that frozen orange juice can?"
Donna: "Can't you see? It says 'concentrate.'"

———

Where do hot dogs dance?
At meatballs.

What are the four seasons?
Salt, pepper, catsup and mayonnaise.

Beth: "Would you like to join me in a cup of tea?"
Veronica: "I don't think we'd both fit."

Mom, entering the kitchen: "I see you've been making chocolate chip cookies."
Marsha: "Can you smell them in the oven already?"
Mom: "No, but I notice M&M shells all over the floor."

How do you repair a broken casserole dish?
With tomato paste.

What ice cream dessert is brown, white and red?
A chocolate sundae with catsup.

What did Mary have for supper?
A little lamb.

Sharon: "You need to make some more ice cubes."
Keith: "Okay. Where's the recipe?"

Liz: "My mom's not a very good cook."
Trish: "Does breakfast taste awful?"
Liz: "No, just weird. She can't even get a pop tart out of the toaster in one piece."

KNOCK-KNOCK JOKES

Knock-knock.
Who's there?
Butcher.
Butcher Who?
Butcher hands up! This is a robbery!

Knock-knock.
Who's there?
Abbey.
Abbey Who?
Abbey birthday to you. . . .

Knock-knock.
Who's there?
Howard.
Howard Who?
Howard is it to lift a piano?

Knock-knock.
Who's there?
Howie.
Howie Who?
Howie gonna win the baseball game
if you won't come out and play!

———

Knock-knock.
Who's there?
Dune.
Dune Who?
Dune anything in particular this afternoon?

———

Knock-knock.
Who's there?
Fanny.
Fanny Who?
Fannybody wants to come out and play, I'm waiting.

———

Knock-knock.
Who's there?
Luke.
Luke Who?
Luke at me twirl my Hoola-Hoop!

Knock-knock.
Who's there?
Matthews.
Matthews Who?
*Matthews are wet. Can I come in
and dwy my socks?*

———

Knock-knock.
Who's there?
Peas.
Peas Who?
Peas open the door and let me in.

———

Knock-knock.
Who's there?
Cinnamon.
Cinnamon Who?
Cinnamon dressed in blue pass by here lately?

———

Knock-knock.
Who's there?
Snakeskin.
Snakeskin Who?
Snakeskin hurtchew, if you ain't keerful.

Knock-knock.
Who's there?
Staten Island.
Staten Island Who?
Staten Island I see out there in the water?

Knock-knock.
Who's there?
Pasta.
Pasta Who?
Pasta gravy, please.

Knock-knock.
Who's there?
Midas.
Midas Who?
Midas well let me in.
I'm not going anywhere.

Knock-knock.
Who's there?
Irish.
Irish Who?
Irish you would open the door.

Knock-knock.
Who's there?
Phillip.
Phillip Who?
Phillip the dog's water bowl, please.
He's very thirsty.

———

Knock-knock.
Who's there?
Tock.
Tock Who?
Tock to me. I'm lonely.

———

Knock-knock.
Who's there?
Rhoda.
Rhoda Who?
Rhoda letter to my mama today.

———

Knock-knock.
Who's there?
Dishes.
Dishes Who?
Dishes Tommy, your besht friend.
Don't you recognishe me?

Knock-knock.
Who's there?
Owl.
Owl Who?
Owl tell you if promise not to reveal my owdentity.

Knock-knock.
Who's there?
Fido.
Fido Who?
Fido known you lived here, I'do come to visit sooner.

Knock-knock.
Who's there?
Wendy.
Wendy Who?
Wendy come looking for me, tell them I'm not here.

Knock-knock.
Who's there?
Celeste.
Celeste Who?
Celeste time I'll ever ask you to come out and play.

71

Knock-knock.
Who's there?
Arthur.
Arthur Who?
Arthur any mean dogs around here?

———

Knock-knock.
Who's there?
Lena.
Lena Who?
Lena little closer. I don't hear too good.

———

Knock-knock.
Who's there?
Watson.
Watson Who?
Watson the grill? I'm hungry.

———

Knock-knock.
Who's there?
Samoa.
Samoa Who?
Samoa ice kweam, pwease.

Knock-knock.
Who's there?
Jamaica.
Jamaica Who?
Jamaica hotdog for me if I asked you to?

———

Knock-knock.
Who's there?
Juneau.
Juneau Who?
Juneau I was your next-door neighbor?

———

Knock-knock.
Who's there?
Ken.
Ken Who?
Ken you come out and play this afternoon?

———

Knock-knock.
Who's there?
Sherwood.
Sherwood Who?
Sherwood like to play with y'all this afternoon.

Knock-knock.
Who's there?
Sam.
Sam Who?
Sam times I think you don't love me lak I love you.

———

Knock-knock.
Who's there?
Sarah.
Sarah Who?
Sarah good way for me to untie this knot!

———

Knock-knock.
Who's there?
Kenya.
Kenya Who?
Kenya gimme a dollar to buy an ice cream cone?

———

Knock-knock.
Who's there?
Turnip.
Turnip Who?
Turnip the stereo, please.

Knock, Knock.
Who's there?
Thumping.
Thumping who?
*Thumping fuzzy and gross is
crawling down your back.*

Knock-knock.
Who's there?
Lettuce.
Lettuce Who?
Lettuce in! It's raining out here!

Knock-knock.
Who's there?
Jess.
Jess Who?
Jess open the door and don't ask questions.

Knock-knock.
Who's there?
Max.
Max Who?
*Max me hungry just smellin' those
hamburgers on the grill.*

Knock-knock.
Who's there?
Telephone.
Telephone Who?
Telephone company. They've made a mistake on our long-distance bill.

———

Knock-knock.
Who's there?
Police.
Police Who?
Police open the door.

———

Knock-knock.
Who's there?
Annette.
Annette Who?
Annette catches more fish than a hook.

———

Knock-knock.
Who's there?
Dishwashing.
Dishwashing Who?
Dishwashing the way I ushed to shpeak before I losht my two front teeth.

GREAT CLEAN JOKES FOR KIDS

Knock-knock.
Who's there?
Moscow.
Moscow Who?
Moscow is brown and pa's cow is black with horns.

Knock-knock.
Who's there?
Alaska.
Alaska Who?
Alaska my dad if I can come outta play.

Knock-knock.
Who's there?
Anita.
Anita Who?
Anita flashlight so I can see in the dark.

Knock-knock.
Who's there?
Theresa.
Theresa Who?
Theresa thunderstorm coming up;
close the windows.

———

Knock-knock.
Who's there?
Noise.
Noise Who?
Noise day, isn't it?

———

Knock-knock.
Who's there?
Adolph.
Adolph Who?
Adolph ball just came in the window.

———

Knock-knock.
Who's there?
Stan.
Stan Who?
Stan back. I'm coming in.

Knock-knock.
Who's there?
Pudding.
Pudding Who?
*Just pudding the final touches
on painting your door.*

Knock-knock.
Who's there?
Abyssinia.
Abyssinia Who?
Abyssinia in church Sunday.

Knock-knock.
Who's there?
Warts.
Warts Who?
Warts the difference between frogs and toads?

Knock-knock.
Who's there?
Sam the drummer.
Beat it.

MUSIC

Adam: "I crossed a dog with a piano student."
Vera: "What did you get?"
Adam: "A dog who's bark was worse than her bite."

———

Who was the spiciest rock 'n' roll
singer of all time?
Elvis Parsley.

———

Claire: "Those are cute bongos you have for ear-
rings. They're so tiny! Can you really play them?"
Brittany: "Yes. Those are my ear drums."
Patrice: "What's a hobo?"
Nicole: "I think it's a wind instrument."

———

Meredith: "I've been playing the piano for five
years now."
Ethan: "Do you ever stop to go to the bathroom?"

———

What did the pianist do after his wrists developed
Carpal Tunnel Syndrome?
Played by ear.

What brass instrument is twice as large as a tuba?

A fourba.

Sheila: "Why does Francis Scott Key get credit for 'The Star-Spangled Banner'?"
Richie: "I guess because he learned all the words before anyone else."

Why was the lemon banned from the orchestra?
It hit too many sour notes.

How do you keep your arm from going to sleep?
Wear a singing wristwatch.

Erskine: "I think I need to clean my tuba."
Band Director: "Try this tuba toothpaste."

———

Patient: "I've swallowed my harmonica."
Doctor: "Good thing you don't play the guitar."

———

"I know a woman who can sing alto and soprano at the same time."
"How does she do that?"
"She has two heads."

———

What's a geologist's favorite kind of music?

Rock.

———

Clive: "It sure was an interesting symphony concert last night. The tuba player's wig slid off into the bowl of his horn!"
Harry: "Oh, no! Did they stop the concert?"
Clive: "No. He just blew his top and went right on playing."

———

Steven: "I wish you sang only Christmas carols."
Mickey: "Why?"
Steven: "Then I'd have to listen to you only one month out of the year."

NEWS

STUDENTS CRASH INTO TREE RETURNING
FROM SCHOOL

———

WOMAN DROWNS IN FOG

———

MYSTERY SOLVED—DROWNED WOMAN
WAS ONLY HIDING

OCCUPATIONS

Reporter: "Do you like your job, sir?"
Astronomer: "Yes. It's heavenly."

———

What sign does a nuclear scientist post on the
office door when he leaves for vacation?
"GONE FISSION."

———

Where do FBI agents go on vacation?
Club Fed.

How do preachers communicate with each other?

Parson to parson.

OCEANS & RIVERS

What was Moby Dick's favorite dinner?

Fish and ships.

Albert: "Do you know what happens when you throw a grey rock into the Red Sea?"

Lon: "It changes color?"

Albert: "No, it gets wet."

The Cantrell family were vacationing aboard a Mississippi River steamboat.

"Is it true," little brother asked the steamboat captain, "that you know every stump and snag on the whole Mississippi River?"

"I sure do," the captain boasted.

Just then the boat ran up on a snag and stopped abruptly.

"There's one," the captain said.

PLAYING

Bart: "Your nose is red. You must've been in the sun too long at the beach yesterday."

Shane: "No I wasn't. I was bobbing for French fries."

Swimmer: "Are there any sharks in this bay?"

Lifeguard: "Not anymore. The crocodiles got 'em."

Jacqui strolled into the kitchen with a brand new baseball.

"Where did you get that?" her mother asked.

"Outside. It was lost."

"Now Jacqui, are you sure it was lost?"

"Yeah, I saw the boy down the street looking for it."

Mother: "Charlie, why aren't you playing ball with your friends?"

Charlie: "Every time it's my turn, they change the rules."

A mother came home to find the living room window broken. "Joel," she called to her son, "do you know anything about this window?"

"Well," Joel said, "I was cleaning my slingshot, and it went off accidentally."

RESTAURANTS

Waitress: "Would you like for me to cut your pizza into four pieces or eight?"
Dawn: "Four. We'd never finish eight."

Waiter: "Did you enjoy your bison steaks?"
Dining family, in unison: "Yes, we enjoyed them very much!"
Waiter: "Good. Here's your buffalo bill."

What's the best way for a guy to propose to a gal at a fast-food restaurant?
With an onion ring.

Two girls went into a fast-food restaurant late one night.
"Have you got anymore cheeseburgers?" asked one.
"Sure," said the clerk.
"Then why did you make so many?"

Walker: "This is not a very good restaurant. I just found a bone."
Suzette: "In your soup?"
Walker: "No, in my lasagna."

Rich Diner: "What's the most expensive soup you have on the menu?"
Waitress: "The one with six carrots in it."

A dog walked into a restaurant, sat down at a table and ordered a cup of coffee.

"That'll be a dollar," the waitress said when she brought the coffee. She added, "You're the first dog I've ever served coffee."

"And at a dollar a cup," said the dog, "I'm sure I'll be the last."

Marsha: "Did you hear about the new café in Paris that sells bag lunches?"
Amy: "No. What's it called?"
Marsha: "The Lunch Bag of Notre Dame."

It was almost closing time, and the ice cream parlor was running very low on supplies when a crowd of teen-agers came in after a soccer game.

"What flavors do you have?" asked one.

"Chocolate, vanilla, strawberry, peach and cherry," said the clerk. "And you can have any one you want, as long as it's vanilla."

Who was the restaurant's star waiter?

Souperman.

Diner: "Waiter, there's a moth in my soup!"
Waiter: "Hmm. The fly must be on vacation."

Amy: "Did you know NASA has opened a café on the surface of the moon?"
Marsha: "Yeah. I heard it has no atmosphere to speak of."

Customer: "What flavors of milkshakes do you sell?"
Waiter, whispering: "Chocolate, vanilla and strawberry."
Customer: "Speak up. Do you have laryngitis?"
Waiter: "Nope. Just chocolate, vanilla and strawberry."

RIDDLES

What word contains three 'e's but only one letter?

Envelope.

What's the most successful thing government has ever invented?

The postage stamp, because it always sticks to its task until completion.

———

What are 10 things in life you can always count on?

Your fingers.

———

What kind of ears do you find on a train engine?

Engineers.

———

What can you break just by calling its name?

Silence.

———

What always seems to be behind time?

A clock face.

———

Why are mushrooms shaped like umbrellas?

Because they grow in damp places.

———

What is cut and spread out on the table but never eaten?

A deck of cards.

What never
asks questions
but gets a lot
of answers?
A doorbell.

Jim was 3 years old on his last birthday
and will be 5 years old on his next birthday.
How can that be?
Today is his 4th birthday.

Why do skeletons stay home every night?
They have no body to go out with.

What word in the English language is usually
pronounced wrong even by scholars?
"Wrong."

What button will you never lose?
Your belly button.

___

What's the best relief for ingrown toenails?
Ingrown toes.

___

Denise: "I know a man who shaves a dozen times a day."
Lindy: "Who in the world is that?"
Denise: "The barber."

___

How do seven cousins divide five potatoes?
Mash them.

___

Teacher: "If the plural of man is men, and the plural of woman is women, what is the plural of child?"
Student: "Twins."

___

What vegetable is a plumber's best friend?
A leek.

___

Teacher: "If four people are standing beneath one umbrella, how many do you think will get wet?"
Student: "Depends on whether it's raining."

91

What's long, sharp and one-eyed?
A needle.

Why were the ten toes nervous?
They were being followed by two heels.

Why are ice cubes kept in the freezer?
To keep the freezer cold.

What gets larger if you take anything away from it?
A hole.

What has a fork and a mouth, but never eats food?
A river.

What's the tiniest room you'll ever find?
A mushroom.

What did one math teacher say to the other?
I've got a problem.

Before the discovery of Australia,
what was the earth's largest island?
Australia.

What's the noblest item ever made from a piece of wood?
A ruler.

Which month has 28 days?
All 12 of them.

How is an apple like a pair of roller skates?
Both have caused the fall of humans.

SCHOOL

Geography Teacher: "Copley, can you tell me where Amsterdam is?"
Copley: "Er—here it is! Page 75!"

A little boy walked up to the teacher's desk and said, "Miss Phillips, I've got bad news for you."
"What is it?" asked Miss Phillips.
"I'm afraid you're in big trouble."
"And why is that?"
"Well, my father says if my grades don't pick up, somebody's in for a beating."

Teacher: "What are zebras good for?"
Student: "To illustrate the letter 'z.'"

Literature Teacher: "Otto, can you tell us who Homer was?"
Otto: "He was Mickey Mantle's sidekick."

Teacher: "How can one child make so many mistakes in one day?"
Student: "By getting up early."

Why did Jerome go to night school?
So he could learn to read in the dark.

Teacher: "What do you call a star with a tail?"
Student: "Mickey Mouse!"

Marcie: "How do you spell 'inneapolis'?"
Slater: "Don't you mean 'Minneapolis?'"
Marcie: "No, I've already got the 'M.'"

Teacher: "Everyone write down the number 11."
Student: "Which 1 comes first?"

Where do numbers take a bath?
In mathtubs.

———

Teacher: "You didn't answer the last two questions on the test."
Student: "Oh. Well, the answers are stuck inside my fountain pen."

———

Lila arrived for her second day of first grade carrying a ladder.

"What's the ladder for?" asked a friend.
"I'm ready for high school," Lila said.

———

Mother: "What did you learn in school today?"
Elena: "We learned to say 'Yes, ma'am' and 'Yes, sir.'"
Mother: "That's wonderful! You'll remember it, won't you?"
Elena: "Yeah, I guess."

———

Teacher: "Do you think it was just as easy to explore the Arctic as it was Antarctica?"
Student: "I don't know. . . . There's a world of difference."

Teacher: "Have you ever read much Shakespeare before now?"
New Student: "I don't think so. Who wrote it?"

Ken: "What are you looking for?"
Kelley: "My earring."
Ken: "I'll help. Where do you think you lost it?"
Kelley: "Down in the science lab."
Ken: "Then why in the world are we looking for it here in the lunchroom?"
Kelley: "The light's much brighter in here."

"What's the capital of Wyoming?"
"That's easy: 'W.'"

What's more difficult than cutting school?
Taping it back together.

What does a school teacher have in common with an eye doctor?
They both stare at pupils.

When do leaves start to turn?
The night before a big test.

GREAT CLEAN JOKES FOR KIDS

Teacher: "Jory, what do you think of Shakespeare's writings?"

Jory: "I think much of what he wrote was a dreadful tragedy."

Teacher: "Warren, can you spell Mississippi?"

Warren: "Do you want me to spell the state or the river?"

Did you hear about the school teacher who was so suspicious while giving tests that his eyes watched each other?

Andy: "The teacher sure kept me busy today."

Michelle: "What was your assignment?"

Andy: "She put me in a round room and told me to sit in the corner."

A student drew a picture of a stage coach with no wheels.

"What holds it up?" asked the teacher.

"Outlaws."

Wally: "I heard you had to stay in at recess. Did the teacher make you write the same sentence over and over?"

Henry: "No. She kept me busy, though."

Wally: "Doing what?"

Henry: "She gave me a piece of paper that said 'See other side.'"

Wally: "So what did it say on the other side?"

Henry: "That side said 'See other side,' too."

Teacher: "Why is Chicago time behind Boston time?"

Student: "Because Boston was discovered first."

The teacher asked Marie, "Please go to the map and locate Cuba."

Marie quickly found Cuba on the map at the front of the room.

"That's good, Marie. Now class, can anyone tell me who discovered Cuba?"

Derek quickly raised his hand. "Marie!"

Teacher: "How many seconds in a minute?"

Don: "Sixty."

Teacher: "That's right. So how many seconds in an hour?"

Don, after a long calculation: "Three-thousand, six-hundred."

Teacher: "Very good! Now, this is a hard one: How many seconds in a year?"

Don: "Twelve."

Teacher: "Twelve? How do you get that?"

Don: "January 2nd, February 2nd, March 2nd. . . ."

Teacher: "Why haven't you turned in your home-work?"

Student: "I accidentally used the paper to make a paper airplane."

Teacher: "Where's the airplane?"

Student: "Somebody skyjacked it."

Teacher: "Kenny, compose a sentence using the word 'archaic.'"

Kenny: "We all know we can't have archaic and eat it, too."

Teacher: "In the Old West, what was cowhide main-ly used for?"

Student: "To keep the cow in one piece?"

Teacher: "Are you having trouble with the test questions?"
Student: "Just with the answers."

Virgil: "How do you spell 'telephone?'"
Shana: "T-e-l-e-p-h-o-n-e. If you would read the dictionary, you would know that yourself."
Virgil: "Hmm. I don't think I want to read the dictionary. I'll wait for the movie."

Teacher: "Robert, how do you spell 'elevate?'"
Robert: "E-l-a-v-a-t."
Teacher: "No, that's not the way it's spelled in the dictionary."
Robert: "You asked me how I spelled it, not the dictionary."

What's the favorite drink of cheerleaders?

Root beer.

"Teacher, I just swallowed my fountain pen!" George screamed.

"Then you may finish the test with your pencil."

———

Teacher: "You missed school yesterday, didn't you?"

Arnold: "No, not much."

———

Perry: "Your lunch box has a glass top. That's neat!"

Tammy: "Yes. When I'm on the bus, I can easily tell whether I'm going to school or going home."

———

Nina came home from school and told her mother, "Our teachers talk to themselves too much."

"Really? Do you think they realize it?"

"Nah. They think students are listening to them."

———

Teacher: "Are you chewing gum?"

New Student: "No, I'm Alison."

———

Teacher: "If you found a dollar in your left trousers pocket and 65 cents in your right pocket, what would you have?"

Student: "Somebody else's britches."

When little Josie came home from her first day at school, her mother asked, "So how do you like school, Josie?"

"Closed," Josie said.

Teacher: "Name three important things that have occurred in the past 25 years."

Rodger: "The space shuttle, the end of the Iron Curtain . . . and me!"

SCIENCE

Where do stars and planets go to school?
At the universe-ity.

Meg: "Did you know there are more than a thousand miles of blood vessels in the human body?"

Peg: "Really? No wonder my dad complains of tired blood."

"How did the new satellite pictures of California turn out?" one NASA scientist asked another.

"Not so good," said the other. "Someone moved."

Teacher: "What's the difference between air and water?"

Student: "Air can get wetter. Water can't."

———

Teacher: "Who was the first brother to fly an airplane at Kitty Hawk, NC? Was it Orville or Wilbur?"

"Orville!" shouted one student.

"Wilbur!" shouted another.

"They're both Wright," said a third.

———

Why were the Wright Brothers first in flight?

Because they weren't wrong.

———

"I didn't understand the science teacher's lesson about the sky today," said Jan.

"Why not?" asked her father.

"It was way over my head."

———

What do you call 4-day-old pizza?

A science project.

SLEEP

"What are you doing in front of the mirror with your eyes closed?"

"I've always wondered what I look like when I'm asleep."

"I can't go to sleep at night," complained Ardie.

"Have you tried counting sheep?" asked Mardie.

"How will that help?"

"It'll bore you, and you'll fall asleep."

A few days later, Mardie asked, "Have you been able to sleep?"

"Nope," said Ardie.

"Did you try counting sheep?"

"Yep. I got up to 3,628."

"Then what happened?"

"Well, then it was time to get up."

What happens if you sleep with a bar of soap under your pillow?

You'll slip out of bed in the morning.

SPORTS

Hoyt: "I think sports are boring."
Bonnie: "Why do you think so?"
Hoyt: "I can always tell you the score before the game even begins."
Bonnie: "Really?"
Hoyt: "Sure. It's 0 to 0."

———

Why do golfers carry extra socks?
In case they get a hole in one.

———

What do four balls mean in baseball?
They mean you can lose three and still be okay.

———

Harry: "Who was the first golfer in history?"
Sherry: "I don't know. Sam Snead?"
Harry: "No—Magellan. He went around in 1519."

———

Reporter: "Why are you a skydiver? Isn't it extremely dangerous jumping out of airplanes?"
Skydiver: "No, jumping is a piece of cake—but it does get risky as you approach the ground."

What did the SCUBA diver find quaking
at the bottom of the bay?
A nervous wreck.

"You'll never make the basketball team," said
Herman. "You're too short."
"But maybe," said Hank, "I could lie about my
height."

Why do hockey players spend
all their time on ice?
*Because their skates would bog
down in the sand.*

Coach: "So you think you know everything there is
to know about soccer?"
New Player: "I do."
Coach: "Then how many holes are in the goal net?"

Ricky: "What's the score of the game?"
Vicky: "17 to 6."
Ricky: "Who's winning?"
Vicky: "17."

STATES

"What's your name?"

"Tex."

"You're from Texas?"

"Nope, Connecticut. I don't like being called 'Con.'"

Rachel: "Did you know the US has four new states?"

Shelby: "You mean, besides Hawaii and Alaska?"

Rachel: "Yes—New Hampshire, New Jersey, New Mexico and New York."

TELEPHONES

"This phone cord's too long," a woman said. "I'm always tripping over it. See what you can do to fix it."

So her husband called the phone company. "Our phone cord's too long," he said. "Pull in about five feet of slack, please."

What happens when you dial 116?
The ambulance rushes to your house upside down.

Why didn't Josie pay her telephone bill?

She believed in free speech.

"Charity, please answer the phone for me!" Mother told Charity.

"Sure," Charity said, running to grab the receiver. "Hello, phone."

"Did you know that certain people who are almost deaf can still use the telephone?" Erin asked.

"No," replied Joey, "but a lot of dumb people certainly use it."

TELEVISION & RADIO

Why did Albert put his radio in the freezer?
He wanted to hear some cool music.

"Are you going to watch the eclipse of the moon tonight?"

"Depends on which channel. We don't get cable TV."

———

Mike: "We just bought a new television set that was made in Japan."

Mark: "Wow! You understand Japanese movies?"

———

Blair: "Sometimes I wonder about Kippie."

Dirk: "Why is that?"

Blair: "He tried to find the English Channel on cable TV."

———

Art: "Did you hear the concert on the radio last night?"

Keri: "My radio won't come on at night."

Art: "What's wrong with it?"

Keri: "It's an AM radio."

———

"My sister doesn't like our new computer."

"Why not?"

"It doesn't get the Disney Channel."

VACATIONS

Henry: "Mom, why are we packing soap in the suitcase?"
Mom: "We'll need it for the trip."
Henry: "But I thought this was supposed to be a vacation."

Brad: "I can get from Philadelphia to Baltimore without buying a ticket."
Joanna: "How?"
Brad: "Walk."

———

Father: "Jack, why did you put a beetle in your sister's sleeping bag?"
Jack: "I couldn't find a snake."

———

Nickie: "I've finally saved up enough money to go to Hawaii!"
Mickie: "Great! When are you going?"
Nickie: "As soon as I save up enough to get back."

———

Randy and Andy visited the beach for the first time in their lives. "Wow! Look at all the water!" Randy shouted.
"Yeah—and that's only the surface!" Andy said.

A troop of girl scouts were huddling around a camp-fire. "Can bears see at night?" Cindy asked nervously.

"I reckon they have to," Wren suggested. "They aren't able to hold flashlights."

———

Trail Guide: "You don't have to worry about riding along those narrow mountain trails. These donkeys are sure-footed critters."

Tourist: "Does that mean when they kick, they don't miss?"

WHAT DO YOU SAY?

What did the low tide say to the high tide?
"Long time no sea."

———

What did the tree say to the logger?
"Leaf me alone."

What did the woman say after she'd stood behind
her car for 10 minutes?
"I'm exhausted."

What was written on the robot's tombstone?
"Rust in peace."

WHAT'S THAT?

What's black and shriveled up and giggles?
A ticklish raisin.

What do you call two bars of soap?
A pair of slippers.

What do you get when you cross a camel with a
station wagon?
A camel that seats nine.

What do you get when you cross a praying mantis
with a termite?
*An insect that returns thanks
before eating your floors.*

What's blue and red and headed
for the doctor's office?
A tomato with frostbite.

What says, "Tick-tock-ruff-ruff"?
A watchdog.

What's long and green and very dangerous?
A herd of charging cucumbers.

What do you get when you cross a
parrot with a grizzly bear?
*Whatever it is, if it says, "Polly wanna cracker,"
you better give it a whole box!*

What's purple and wears a mask?
The Lone Grape.

What's the opposite of minimum?
Minipop.

What's long and yellow and
helps elderly ladies across the street?
Banana Scouts.

What do you get when you cross a
woodpecker and a carrier pigeon?
A bird that knocks before delivering the message.

What has one head and four legs?
A bed.

———

What's yellow, has four doors and lies on its back?
A sick taxicab.

———

What do you get when you cross a
rooster and a bull?
Roost beef.

———

What's hairy and sneezes?
A peach with a cold.

———

What do you call a young fox after it's
30 days old?
Thirty-one days old.

———

What has three heads, two arms, two wings, eight
legs and two tails?
A horseback rider carrying a falcon.

What animal sees just as well from one end as the other?

A blind one.

———

What hops around holding up banks?
A robbit.

———

What's purple and goes, "Slam! Slam!"?
A two-door grape.

WISDOM & WISECRACKS

Reporter: "Have you lived in Johnson County all your life?"
Old-timer: "Not yet."

What does the president do with his cabinet?

Keeps his china in it.

___

What's the hardest thing about
learning to ice skate?

Ice.

___

Fireflies are pretty bright,
for such little critters.

WORK

"Did you hear Harry went to work at the bank?"
"No. Why does he want to work at a bank?"
"He heard there's money in it."

___

Boss: "You drive nails like lightning."
Carpenter: "Pretty fast, huh?"
Boss: "Nope. You never hammer the same place
twice."

___

Why did the weather announcer quit her job?
She didn't find the weather very agreeable.

Molly: "Why did your father go to work at the
bakery?"

Allie: "He kneads the dough."

Will: "I just heard they aren't building railroad
tracks any longer."

Sam: "Why not?"

Will: "They're already long enough."

ODDS & ENDS

Why won't a bicycle stand up
when it's not moving?
It's two-tired.

Two walls were talking to each other when a man
overheard them and shouted, "Be quiet!"

"Come on," one wall whispered softly to the other.
"I'll meet you at the corner and we can finish our
discussion."

Why did Miriam put a bag of ice
under her aunt's easy-chair?
She wanted to see Auntie freeze.

117

Carey: "You sure have a weird name."
Bretopnius: "It's better than the one my father first pulled out of the hat."
Carey: "What was that?"
Bretopnius: "Eight-and-a-Quarter."

Mother: "Has Clay finished changing that light bulb yet?"
Billy: "I don't think so. He keeps breaking them accidentally with the hammer."

———

Why did Lindy carry her umbrella to school!
She didn't want to leave it home alone.

———

Jamie's kitten had climbed high up a tree, and it wouldn't come down, no matter how long she coaxed. "What can we do?" she asked her father.
"Wait until September. He'll catch the first leaf that falls and float right to the ground."

———

What cowboy wears a black mask just like the Lone Ranger's, rides a horse just like Silver and has a sidekick who could be Tonto's twin brother?
The Clone Ranger.

What's the opposite of subway jam?
Forest preserve.

———

Why do artists sign their paintings?
So you can tell which edge is the bottom.

———

Wendy: "Don't you ever file your nails?"
Mindy: "No, I usually put them in the trash can."

———

Winona: "Did you hear the McMillans are moving to Gettysburg?"
Andrea: "No. Why are they moving?"
Winona: "Because they want to have a Gettysburg address."

———

How did the cat succeed in winning a starring role in a movie?
With purr-sistency.

———

Morris: "Did you hear about the skeleton who became a movie star?"
Glenda: "How did he do that?"
Morris: "He had good connections."

Fran: "Why does your family have a mirror on the bathroom ceiling?"

Dan: "So we can see ourselves gargle."

How do barbers finish their work so fast?

With shortcuts.

Gavin: "How do you pronounce t-o?"

Grady: "To."

Gavin: "What about t-w-o?"

Grady: "Two."

Gavin: "And how do you pronounce the second day of the week?"

Grady: "Tuesday."

Gavin: "Wrong. It's Monday."

Why did the fireman phone the police?
He saw the fire escape.

What did the secretary do with her
old fingernails?
She filed them away.

What do you call an acorn on a spaceship?
An astronut.

Mother: "You're not being selfish with the sled, are
you Jenny? You're letting your little sister use it half
the time?"
Jenny: "Yes, ma'am. I use it coming down the hill
and she uses it going up."

A boy phoned the police department and reported, "I
can't find my goldfish!"
"That sounds like a problem for the Navy, not us,"
said the dispatcher.

If joy is the opposite of misery,
what's the opposite of woe?
Giddy-up.

A woman sat down on a park bench beside a little girl. "And what's your name?" she asked with a smile.

"Irene."

"Irene who?"

"Irene Go to Your Room."

Why did the Invisible Man have no children?
Because he was not apparent.

Marshall: "I know I've seen your face somewhere. . ."
Marti: "Well, it's always been right here on my head."

"Mommy, is pollution worse in the cities?"
"I'm afraid so, dear."
"Then why don't they build cities in the country?"

What are the three main causes of accidental fires?
Men, women and children.

What do you call a 12-inch roller-coaster?
A ruler-coaster.

Brother: "It's a good thing we weren't born in Greece."

Sister: "Why not?"

Bother: "We've never learned to read and write Greek."

Where do astronauts bathe?

In meteor showers.

Morey: "I've discovered a quick way to double my money."

Amy: "How's that?"

Morey: "I fold it in half."

What sound do Hawaiians make when they laugh?
A low "ha."

Brandy: "I've just figured out how to come away from Las Vegas with a small fortune!"
Randy: "How?"
Brandy: "Go there with a large fortune!"

———

Dave: "I'm thinking of asking Stephanie out for a date again."
Mickey: "Wow! You mean you've dated Stephanie before?"
Dave: "No, but I've thought of asking her out before."

———

Mother: "How would you like to take your cold medicine?"
Son: "With a fork."

———

Wren: "My cat can jump higher than a barn."
Lynn: "I guess so. Barns can't jump."

A man walked up to the ticket office at a train station and asked, "How long will the next train be?" "About 120 cars," said the agent.

———

Mother: "Charlie, you're soaking wet. Didn't you take your umbrella to school?"
Charlie: "Yes, ma'am."
Mother: "Well, it didn't keep you very dry."
Charlie: "No, ma'am. But it wasn't the umbrella's fault. I fell in the lake."

———

James: "We went to a movie last night and I cried through the whole thing."
LaVonne: "Was it really that sad?"
James: "No. I just kept thinking about how much money we paid to get in."
Judge: "You're hereby sentenced to 200 years."
Prisoner: "Thanks, Your Honor. I was afraid it would be a life sentence."

———

Walt: "I'm looking for a man with one arm named Pete."
Will: "What's the name of his other arm?"

Why did the candle go insane?

Birthday burn-out.

Who wears a black mask and always smells great?

The Cologne Ranger.